ideals® EASTER

More Than 50 Years of Celebrating Life's Most Treasured Moments

Vol. 57, No. 1

"Spring came that year like magic and like music and like song."
—Thomas Wolfe

IDEALS—Vol. 57, No. 1 January 2000 IDEALS (ISSN 0019-137X) is
published six times a year: January, March, May, July, September, and November by
IDEALS PUBLICATIONS INCORPORATED,
535 Metroplex Drive, Suite 250, Nashville, TN 37211.
Periodical postage paid at Nashville, Tennessee, and additional mailing offices.
Copyright © 2000 by IDEALS PUBLICATIONS INCORPORATED.
POSTMASTER: Send address changes to Ideals, PO Box 305300,
Nashville, TN 37230. All rights reserved.

Title IDEALS registered U.S. Patent Office.
SINGLE ISSUE—U.S. $5.95 USD; Higher in Canada
ONE-YEAR SUBSCRIPTION—U.S. $19.95 USD; Canada $36.00 CDN (incl. GST and shipping); Foreign $25.95 USD
TWO-YEAR SUBSCRIPTION—U.S. $35.95 USD; Canada $66.50 CDN (incl. GST and shipping); Foreign $47.95 USD

ISBN 0-8249-1159-8   GST 131903775

Cover Photo
Yellow Tulips
Photograph by
Nancy Matthews

Inside Front Cover
LES IRIS DE GUEMAPPE
Heliette Wzgarda, artist
The Grand Design, Leeds,
England/Superstock

Inside Back Cover
A YOUNG GIRL PICKING FLOWERS
Marianne Stokes, artist
Christie's Images/Superstock

Joy

Oscar Wilde

Already the slim crocus stirs the snow,
And soon yon blanched fields will bloom again
With nodding cowslips for some lad to mow.
For with the first warm kisses of the rain,
The winter's icy sorrow breaks to tears,
And the brown thrushes mate, and with
    bright eyes the rabbit peers
From the dark warren where the fir cones lie
And treads one snowdrop under foot and runs
Over the mossy knoll, and blackbirds fly
Across our path at evening, and the suns
Stay longer with us; ah, how good to see
Grass-girdled Spring in all her joy
    of laughing greenery!

*Can words describe the fragrance
of the very breath of spring?*
—Neltje Blanchan

A necklace of snow adorns the year's first crocus in Bristol, New Hampshire. Photo by William Johnson/Johnson's Photography.

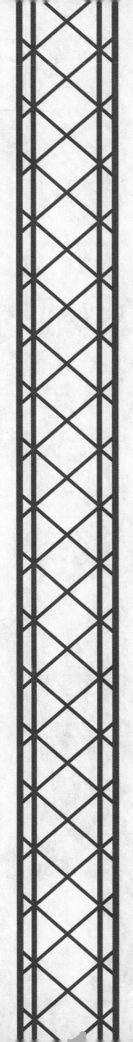

So Small a Thing

Joy Belle Burgess

Could it have been so small a thing
That I have heard a wild bird sing
And wake the early light of dawn
With its sweet, exultant song?

Could it have been so small a thing
That I have breathed the breath of spring
Where violets perfume the air
And bid my heart to linger there?

Could it have been so small a thing
That I have heard the forest ring
With hymns that ripple through the trees
And whisper only words of peace?

Could it have been so small a thing
That I have seen a sign of spring;
For each wee flower and forest tree
Has taught my heart new songs to sing.

Spring's Gifts

Virginia Blanck Moore

Spring has gifts for everyone—
    rain-washed air and golden sun,
    songs of birds to greet the day,
    skies turned palest blue from gray.

Spring has gifts from morn till night—
    extra hours of welcome light,
    budlets covering branches bare,
    new life springing everywhere.

But perhaps her greatest gift
    is the heart's and spirit's lift
    as weary-winter souls relearn
    that springtime always does return.

LEFT: A well-tended garden in northern Illinois explodes with spring color. Photo by Jessie Walker. OVERLEAF: An Oregon garden thrives with iris and lupine. Photo by Steve Terrill.

DEAR MARCH

Emily Dickinson

Dear March, come in!
How glad I am!
I looked for you before,
Put down your hat—
You must have walked—
How out of breath you are!
Dear March, how are you?
And the rest?
Did you leave Nature well?
Oh, March, come right upstairs with me,
I have so much to tell!

I got your letter, and the bird's;
The maples never knew
That you were coming till I called;
I declare, how red their faces grew!
But, March, forgive me—
And all those hills
You left for me to hue;
There was no purple suitable,
You took it all with you.

Who knocks? That April!
Lock the door!
I will not be pursued!
He stayed away a year, to call
When I am occupied.
But trifles look so trivial
As soon as you have come,
That blame is just as dear as praise
And praise as mere as blame.

A Missouri pond is edged by blooming daffodils and crabapple limbs. Photo by Gay Bumgarner.

Springtime Symphony

You'll hear them soon, the peepers' rhythmic peals as they pierce the stillness of the ponds and pools. I listen every year as, in the first warm days and mild nights, the tree frogs' symphony resounds from the marshes, swamps, and bogs.

Each year, I wait with the same anticipation for that warm afternoon of sun and the mild, soft evening when the tree frogs known as hylas usher in the touch of spring with their resonating pipes. I never tire of listening to their shrill flutes. I like to think that this springtime symphony is surrounded by the golden glow of the moon and the silvery sheen of the stars.

I have heard the hylas as early as February, but late March or April usually brings their pealing sounds to their peak. The first few feeble notes usually catch my attention in the late afternoon. Then as twilight appears and slips on into the deepening darkness, the chorus of peepers intensifies. The ponds and swamps seem to be covered with echoing peals that every wave and ripple of the waters carries into the night.

Each year, I wait for the sounds of the peepers as eagerly as I wait for the first liquid warble of the bluebird in the orchard on the hill, or the "o-ka-lee" of the redwing in the swamp with its reeds and cattails. My heart thrills to hear the hylas just as it does to hear the robin's first carol from the roadside maple or to discover the song of cascading waterfalls after the breakup of ice in the creek.

To me, the marshland concert of the peepers is as joyous as any of the year's musical performances. It is one of the many heralds of spring. And I hope the peepers continue their piping peals so that I can continue to listen and enjoy the welcoming of spring.

The author of three published books, Lansing Christman has been contributing to Ideals for almost thirty years. Mr. Christman has also been published in several American, foreign, and braille anthologies. He lives in rural South Carolina.

An Eastern gray tree frog finds a colorful place to rest. Photo by Gay Bumgarner.

The Spring Is Here

Louise Chandler Moulton

I miss you, Sweet! The spring is here;
The young grass trembles on the leas;
The violet's breath enchants the breeze,
And the blue sky bends low and near.
Home-coming birds, with carol clear,
Make their new nests in budding trees.
I miss you, Sweet, now spring is here,

And young grass trembles on the leas.
You were my spring, and spring is dear;
Without you can the Maytime please?
Let lavish June withhold her fees,
And winter reign throughout the year—
I miss you, Sweet, though spring is here.

Spring Road

Sheila Stinson

There is a road that holds the breath of spring—
Pale apple-blossoms for remembering,
A bluebird's vivid wings against the sky,
A thin small wind through lilac bloom, a sigh
As subtle as the touch of tender lips
Whispering secrets through the trees' tall tips.

Gay dew-drenched morning glories,
 blue and white,
Lifting their small round faces to the light.

And always down this road remembering
I walk with you—glad for another spring.

A woodland path weaves through the trees in Pine Mountain, Georgia. Photo by William Johnson/Johnson's Photography.

Spring Fever

Mrs. Merrill D. Spencer

My spirit is buoyant and free as the air;
My heart holds no memory of sorrow;
I feel no regret for things of the past
And a blithe unconcern for tomorrow.

I bask in the sunshine, contented and still,
Yet aware of the robin's bold wooing;
The spring surges over my winter-logged soul—
A tonic of nature's own brewing.

Spring

Gail Brook Burket

The bright commotion of the spring
Perplexes me.
Green leaves pop out on every tree
Vivaciously.

The sun pours down its torrid gold;
The south wind drills
The chorus lines of daffodils
In yellow frills.

The birds tend nests and loudly sing;
The fledglings grow.
Industrious bees buzz to and fro
The tulip row.

Oh, everything has vigor, vim,
Vitality,
And most excessive energy,
Excepting me!

Friends enjoy the spring sun in Carl Larsson's WOMAN LYING ON A
BENCH. *Image from Musée du Louvre, Paris, Lauros-Giraudon,
Paris/Superstock.*

Remember When

THE MAIL-ORDER CATALOG

Marjorie Holmes

"Look children, see what's come in the mail," I summoned my young one day. "A big, fat mail-order catalog!"

They rushed up to see what I was so pleased about. And reacted with about as much enthusiasm as if I'd just presented them with a big, fat telephone directory. Its plethora of riches failed to impress them—they see all this and more in store windows every day. . . . Politely they listened to my promises that when the catalog got a little older I'd let them cut it up for paper dolls—and escaped.

Somewhat saddened, I stood sniffing its elusive, nostalgic scent of thin, inky pages and thick, glossy ones. Letting myself be whisked back to the days when the arrival of mail-order catalogs signaled spring and fall. Like spying your first robin or a scarlet maple leaf. *Sears and Roebuck. Montgomery Ward.* What magical words! For if you lived in a small town or the country, they brought the whole thrilling world to your door.

This was important in several ways. Snowbound much of the winter, without much choice in merchandise in the few available stores, these vast packages of print and pictures spread before dazzled eyes almost everything known to the needs of man. Entire families were often clothed and outfitted from their pages, from a baby's first diapers on through the wedding dress. Whole houses were furnished by mail—curtains, rugs, parlor suite, nickel-plated stove, and even the kitchen sink. But more, the catalog was a source of information, of contact, a glimpse of fabulous people at work and play. A springboard for hope, the touchstone of dreams.

We children fought over turns to explore it, lying enrapt on the floor. The tissue-thin pages rustled as you turned them, like the whisper of young leaves; the shiny colored ones held the vivid promise of rainbows. . . . We spent thousands of nonexistent dollars fervently filling out blanks from old ones as we "ordered" the most expensive items—furniture, jewelry, furs.

Though Mother too faithfully studied and loved her catalogs, she seldom sent away for things. "It's hard to tell how things really look from a picture," she said. "And besides you can't always be sure they'll fit. Also," she reasoned, "we should support our hometown merchants. They've been good to us." ("Good to us" meant letting us have credit when times were hard.) We found her attitude frustrating, in view of this surefire magic. She didn't have many clothes, and my sister and I longed desperately to send away and get her a dress.

A dress was simply beyond our means, even after weeks of saving, so we decided to settle for a hat. We picked out the prettiest we could find, not a very big hat, but one richly adorned with fruit and flowers. Eagerly we filled out the order blank, stealthily emptying our banks and slipping off to the post office to buy a money order. We could hardly wait. We wanted it in time for Easter. Our suspense was agonizing as the weeks slipped by. Every time she longingly fingered a hat downtown, or spoke about trimming an old one, we were tempted to tell her.

At last, a few days before Easter, the mail truck stopped before our house. As the driver marched up the walk and knocked we thought we would explode. "But we didn't order anything!" Mother protested, even as we began to shout: "Surprise! Surprise!" Baffled, she opened the box, lifted it out of the tissue paper, and there it was in all its glory. Even more gorgeous than we imagined, rosy and shiny and velvet-ribboned, a veritable cornucopia of fruit and flowers.

"Oh, my!" Mother exclaimed, looking slightly dismayed. She picked it up gingerly, turning it around on her hand. "This is for *me?*" She'd never

A young girl carefully selects from the wonders offered in a mail-order catalog. Image from H. Armstrong Roberts.

worn anything but the plainest hats; obviously she was almost too overcome with joy to speak.

She went at once to the mirror and put it on, with some difficulty, over her generous mounds of hair. . . . Until that moment it had never occurred to us that the hat might not become her. In our loving dreams she would be transformed before our eyes into a likeness of one of those dream-creatures of the catalog.

Instead, Mother turned to us looking stricken—half sad, half amused. "Oh, girls, girls, it's the most beautiful hat in the world!" she cried, embracing us. "Just wait, I'll curl my hair Saturday night and Sunday I'll have my powder on. It'll look just—fine!"

It did. It almost did. We all complimented her vastly when she was ready for church, and so did her friends when she got there. But something was wrong and we knew it, with a queer wrench in the region of our stomachs. . . .

Mother loyally wore the hat—how long I don't recall. After a while it didn't look funny on her anymore; it simply became a part of her, like her dependable blue crepe dress. When its flowers began to wilt, its fruit to wither, she even doctored them up and wore it some more. She was actually regretful when at last she was forced to abandon it. "I'll never forget this hat," she said, and she spoke for all of us.

I think of it now on that rare occasion when a catalog comes in the mail. . . . I thought of it as I tried to rouse in my children the sense of delight that a catalog used to bring. But a catalog cannot be the passport to wonder to them that it was to us.

No, really to thrill to the magic of a catalog you must live in the country or a little town. And be a pigtailed dreamer in the days when winters were long and lonely, and a hat was truly a hat to be worn lengthily, head high, by a mother who loved her little girls.

BITS & PIECES

At Easter let your clothes be new,
Or else be sure you will it rue.
—Proverb

A gush of birdsong, a patter of dew,
A cloud and a rainbow's warning,
Suddenly sunshine and perfect blue—
An April day in the morning.
—Harriet Prescott Spofford

On Easter morn she kneels and prays,
A gentle saint in baby blue—
Forgive her that her hat is new,
And all those dear, coquettish ways.
—Louise Chandler Moulton

Each day comes bearing its gifts; untie the ribbons.
—Ann Ruth Schabacker

'Twas Easter Sunday. The full-blossomed trees
Filled all the air with fragrance and with joy.
—Henry Wadsworth Longfellow

Her feet beneath her petticoat
Like little mice stole in and out,
As if they feared the light;
But, oh, she dances such a way,
No sun upon an Easter day
Is half so fine a sight.
—Sir John Suckling

In your Easter bonnet,
With all the frills upon it,
You'll be the grandest lady
In the Easter parade.
—Irving Berlin

Can there be any day but this,
Though many suns to shine endeavor?
We count three hundred, but we miss:
There is but one, and that one ever.
—George Herbert

I think of the garden after the rain,
And hope to my heart comes singing.
At morn the cherry blooms will be white,
And the Easter bells be ringing!
—Edna D. Proctor

Spring bursts today,
For Christ is risen, and all the earth's at play.
—Christina Rossetti

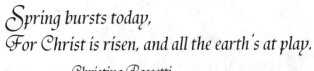

April Winds

Michael Lewis

In spring the day is early
And wakes a rosy world
Where all the twigs are pearly
And every bud's uncurled.
The birds are up and singing
Before they can be seen,
And April winds are winging
Their way to make earth green.

In spring the sun grows pleasant
To prove that he is fond.
He scatters for a present
Gold pieces in each pond.
He sets the bell-flowers ringing
With perfumed melodies,
And April winds run swinging
Among the startled trees.

American artist Donald Zolan finds a pair of brave climbers in Two in a Tree.
Image copyright © Zolan Fine Arts, Ltd., Hershey, Pennsylvania.

Children are God's apostles,

day by day sent forth

to preach of love

and hope

and peace.

—James Russell Lowell

CHILD ON A SUNDAY MORNING

Geraldine Ross

Her stained-glass courtesy enchants the hour,
A morning attitude, an eight o'clock
As luminous, as new as light itself.
Devotion scrubbed and in a starched new frock,
Its heart a hymn, its innocence a prayer,
Its Bible-text enthusiasm, gold
In earth's collection plate. This wide-eyed psalm
Makes us who have been dulled and lost and old
Not dusty-hearted now, not looking down
But wearing all our Sundays like a crown!

CATHEDRALS

Grace V. Watkins

Not all cathedrals stand upon a hill
Or close beside a crowded city square;
For I have walked with children when the still
Enfolding vesper hour was blue and fair
And, pausing, seen cathedral towers rise
Within their wondering, faith-lighted eyes.

And sometimes, kneeling with them, I have heard
Cathedral chimes within their murmured prayer,
So bright with loveliness my heart was stirred
As though a host of angels lingered near,
And in that sanctuary, glory-aisled,
Looked on in holy quietness and smiled.

Fellowship begins as the morning assembly ends in AFTER SERVICE *by artist Leo Carty Fincher. Image copyright Arts Uniq Inc., Cookeville, Tennessee.*

April Rain

Sylvia Trent Auxier

Along the sloping roof-expanse
The April raindrops glide and glance,
Stitch back and forth in harmony

The downy darkness over me,
And quilt a gay design that seems
A tulip pattern for my dreams.

April Rain

Jessie Wilmore Murton

There is no sweeter smell than April rain
Upon fresh earth,
Flinging bright javelins into green sod,
Waking to birth
The life that waits
In every bud and blade and furrowed clod.

There is no music soothing to the soul
As April rain,
Washing away all winter's soot and grime,
Bringing again
Fulfillment of a faith it holds
Against all loss, all heartache, and all time.

Spring Rain

Stella Tremble

Dancing raindrops, shiny, swift,
Through the air they bound and sift
With a whizzy, whirry hum,
Skipping, slipping down the street.
Like a thousand bees they come,
With a whizzy, whirry hum.

Violet, trillium wake up!
Let the raindrops fill your cup!
As they fall in silver spray,
To your roots they find their way.
Springtime comes in slanting rain
Dashing on the windowpane.

A family of pastel hyacinths enjoys a drink of spring rain in Bristol, New Hampshire. Photo by William Johnson/Johnson's Photography.

BASKETS

Samantha J. Noonan

Thirty-two years ago, my husband and I bought a tiny old farmhouse on a quiet country road. The house had two small loft bedrooms on the upper level and, downstairs, a great room with living areas encircling a brick center chimney. The floors were wide planks of pine, and the low ceilings were made of hand-hewn beams more than a century old. The house was a good fit for the two of us. All around us stretched a neighbor's hay fields, and beautiful tree-covered hills rose in the distance. We imagined that this little house would be the perfect starting place for our life together. We also imagined that, when the time came to add children to our family, we would move on to something bigger. I remember our first night in the house. As I sat in the kitchen unpacking boxes, I discovered an old nail in one of the ceiling beams—a wedge-shaped, black, headless nail protruding an inch or so from the wood. On it I hung a basket my mother had given me when I'd first left home. She'd always called it a "gizzard basket"; it was oval shaped, wider on the bottom than the top, with a circular opening on the side. I couldn't find another home for the basket in the cramped kitchen, so I hung it absentmindedly on the nail, thinking I would move it once we were settled. The basket still hangs from that nail, and we still live in that old farmhouse. Sometimes life just doesn't follow the plans we make for it.

More than anything else, it is this old house that has made me into a collector of baskets. I just kept discovering more old nails in the beams. Of course we hung other things from them: herbs, keys, children's wet mittens (yes, the children did come, and no, they did not drive us to a newer, bigger home); but baskets have always seemed most at home on those antique nails. Their warm, honey-brown tones are an ideal complement to the dark, weathered beams. So I began a collection. Not the type of collection meant to be an investment or a showcase, but a collection that grew slowly and unconsciously until it became as much a part of my home as the boards on the floor and the beams on the ceiling.

I have found my baskets everywhere, from yard sales to antique shops to craft fairs. Friends and family noticed my collection early on, and for years I have received baskets at every gift-giving occasion. One Christmas my mother gave me a beautiful old handmade pea basket. It is a low-sided, oblong basket perfect for gathering vegetables from the garden. This type of basket was originally made for bringing in black-eyed peas from gardens in the Deep South; I have used mine mainly for green beans and tomatoes. When my daughters were little, they used it as a cradle for their dolls. Another favorite basket was a gift from my eldest daughter on Mother's Day. It came with a hand-picked bouquet of flowers from the garden in her first home. This one is dedicated to my own springtime cuttings. I have baskets made of splints from oak and ash trees and others woven from willow and palm. They take every imaginable shape and size; and most, at one time or another, have served a practical purpose in my day-to-day life. When every nail in the old beams was full, I pounded in new ones.

We never did outgrow this old house; rather it stretched and grew to meet our needs. We turned the upstairs lofts into three complete bedrooms. We updated the bathrooms. We papered and painted and sanded and refinished. And in the old kitchen, where I sat all those years ago unpacking, where I hung that first basket thinking only of getting it out of the way, baskets now crawl across the beams like vines. If I sit in the kitchen on a quiet evening, each one offers me a piece of memory, a slice of life from our many happy years here.

I didn't plan on becoming a collector of baskets, just like I didn't plan on squeezing a family of four into this old farmhouse. But today, I couldn't imagine any other home for my family, and my family couldn't imagine home without baskets.

BASKET WEAVINGS

If you would like to collect baskets, the following information will be helpful:

BASKET STYLES

• The pea basket is long and low, designed for gathering black-eyed peas.

• The cotton basket is tall and wide. On cotton plantations, these baskets were left at the end of rows. Pickers gathered the crop in sacks and then deposited full sacks into the basket.

• The Hickey basket was handcrafted by a Native American who went by the name Hickey. He traveled the backroads of rural Tennessee in the early 1900s and traded his hand-woven willow baskets for food. These are rare today and treasured by collectors.

• The goose basket is shaped liked a spittoon and was used to cover the head of a goose while his feathers were plucked.

• The Nantucket lightship basket was made by sailors serving long tours of duty at the lighthouse off of Nantucket Island in the late nineteenth and early twentieth centuries.

• Cheese or shellfish baskets are rare. They feature an open weave and a circular pattern and were used in cheese making or to carry shellfish.

BASKET MATERIALS AND CONSTRUCTION

• Baskets have been made from oak, ash, hickory, black elm, willow, bamboo, palm, flax, reeds, honeysuckle, pine needles, yucca, cattails, and almost any material that an artisan can make into strips.

• Collectors can tell the type of wood by studying the basket's color, grain, and even scent. Aged white ash appears smooth and light; black ash ages to a nut brown color. Hickory takes on a silver-gray tone, as does oak, but the former can be identified by its close, even grain. Sweet grass baskets, when damp, will retain some of their sweet scent, even after years of aging.

• There are four basic methods of basket making: wickerwork, twining, plaiting, and coiling. The

A unique rack displays a collection of antique baskets. Photo by Jessie Walker.

first three are variations of using a flexible weaving material and rigid spokes. Coiling is more specialized, using long spirals of material stitched together with a grass wrapping.

COLLECTING AND CARE

• Older baskets are generally more valuable than newer; the exception are some fine modern baskets made by skilled artisans.

• Unscrupulous dealers will falsely age baskets, so buyers should be educated.

• Willow baskets are generally the least expensive and the easiest to find.

• Clean antique baskets with a mild soap and warm water. After soaping, wipe gently with a damp sponge. Rub dry, brittle baskets with a mixture of linseed oil and turpentine.

From My Garden Journal

Deana Deck

LILY OF THE VALLEY

Finding tiny lily-of-the-valley blossoms can be as difficult as finding a hint of spring at the end of a long winter—unless you follow your nose! On a visit to my brother's farm in the southeastern tip of Virginia one year, I took a stroll up an overgrown lane that led into a wooded area. Suddenly I became aware of the most delightful scent wafting on the breeze. I couldn't identify it, so I began searching for the source. I expected it to emanate from an exotic tropical vine, perhaps, but saw only gnarled wild grapes hanging from the trees. No flowering shrubs were in sight, no stands of fragrant narcissus or twisted ropes of honeysuckle.

Mystified, I left the trail and wandered into the woods where I came upon the source of the captivating scent. Near the ruins of an old springhouse was a vast green mass of wide-leafed ground cover, and nestled between the leaves were racemes bearing the creamy-white, bell-shaped blossoms of the delicate lily of the valley (*Convallaria majalis*).

Since the lily-of-the-valley plant grows wild in the mountains of the southeast United States from Virginia to South Carolina, those plants I found growing around the deserted springhouse may have colonized the area on their own. But portions of my brother's farmhouse have been dated to the late 1700s, so it's easy to picture an early pioneer housewife finding a clump of these fragrant flowers in the woods and moving a few to line the path leading to her springhouse.

On her daily visits to retrieve milk or butter, she might have enjoyed their heady fragrance; and as the plants multiplied from year to year, she no doubt harvested the aromatic blooms for use in sachets and potpourris since the plant is easily dried for use in arrangements. If she had access to either fine sand or a mix of borax and cornmeal, our imaginary homemaker could have placed the blossoms, with a good length of stem, into the dessicant and preserved them to brighten up her cabin during the dark winter days.

Today, lilies of the valley remain a favorite with gardeners who appreciate their simple elegance and rich scent. Although they are members of the lily family, these hardy spring bloomers grow from rhizomes instead of bulbs and flourish in shady, moist areas. Cultivation is simple if you get the plants off to a good start by amending the soil in the planting bed. A deep, rich mix of compost and sand will keep your lily-of-the-valley bed productive for years. Dappled shade and moist soil are the other two requirements.

Lily-of-the-valley foliage begins to die down in mid- to late-summer and becomes unattractive. You can either clip it back, which can be time-consuming once it has become widely spread, or you can hide it. Planting lily of the valley amid an

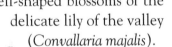

existing ground cover of ivy or vinca minor will help disguise the fading foliage at summer's end. Lily of the valley also does well planted next to hostas and ferns, both of which enjoy the same growing conditions: shade and moist soil.

When setting out the plants, place them about six inches apart, and mulch them well if hard winters are common in your area. The plants are hardy to Zone 4, where temperatures can drop as low as −30°, and freezing is not a problem as much as thawing. Mulching helps protect the plants by preventing sudden thaws in late winter which can force roots out of the ground. Mulch maintains moisture and holds the soil at an even temperature all winter.

To facilitate watering, run a soaker hose among the plants before applying the mulch. When dry weather arrives, the hose will make watering a simple matter of turning on the faucet and letting the water run for a couple of hours each week. This technique will also protect your fragile ferns and hostas from summer dry spells.

Once you have established a thriving bed of creamy-white lily of the valley blooms, you may wish to add a few of the unique pink variety called *Convallaria majalis Rosea*. Only recently developed by breeders, *Rosea* is still somewhat difficult to find, but a reputable garden center or catalog should be able to help you.

In their natural environment, lilies of the valley bloom from mid-May to mid-June, but you can easily force them indoors for earlier blooms by using a bowl filled with moist fiber, peat moss, or sand. The roots need to experience about a week of freezing weather, and in cold climates can be pot-

> *I often remember a hymn sung in Sunday service when I was a child: "He's the lily of the valley, the bright and morning star. He's the fairest of ten thousand to my soul."*

ted and left outdoors until three or four weeks before blooms are desired. The rhizomes can also be placed in the freezer for five or six days and then planted in pots, watered, and placed in good light. If you live in the Deep South where the soil seldom freezes and want outdoor blossoms, you'll have to be content with forcing the rhizomes in containers and moving them onto the porch or patio for a brief center-stage appearance. It's well worth the effort to be able to enjoy the heady scent.

Oftentimes as I enjoy the lily of the valley's aroma and beauty, I also hear music. Not just any music, but a line from a hymn often sung in Sunday service when I was a child: "He's the lily of the valley, the bright and morning star. He's the fairest of ten thousand to my soul." In fact, the lily of the valley is sometimes used in religious references, and another traditional name for the plant is Our Lady's Tears, which makes the plant seem an appropriate choice for the Easter table. Although the plant's normal bloom time falls after the Easter season, forcing the blooms inside allows you to enjoy them earlier. You may want to try transplanting a small clump of blooms into empty eggshells that have been dyed, hollowed, and placed into decorative egg cups. Then place one small bouquet at each place setting. With each glance at the lilies' bell-shaped blossoms and every sniff of their luxurious scent, your Easter Sunday guests are sure to be reminded of the wonders of spring.

Deana Deck tends to her flowers, plants, and vegetables at her home in Nashville, Tennessee, where her popular garden column is a regular feature in The Tennessean.

EASTER EVE

Anne Bethel Spencer

If ever a garden was Gethsemane,
With old tombs set high against
The crumpled olive tree and lichen,
This, my garden has been to me.
For such as I none other is so sweet:
Lacking old tombs, here stands my grief,
And certainly its ancient tree.

Peace is here and in every season
A quiet beauty.
The sky falling about me
Evenly to the compass. . .
What is sorrow but tenderness now
In this earth-close frame of land and sky
Falling constantly into horizons
Of east and west, north and south;
What is pain but happiness here
Amid these green and wordless patterns,
Indefinite texture of blade and leaf:

Beauty of an old, old tree,
Last comfort in Gethsemane.

*If we cannot find God . . . in the bursting seed or
opening flower, I do not think we should discern
him any more on the grass of Eden or beneath the
moonlight of Gethsemane.*

—*James Martineau*

*A wagon holds spring bulbs in a private garden in Lacanada, California.
Photo by Charles Benes/FPG International.*

Devotions
FROM THE Heart

Pamela Kennedy

Jesus said, "Father, forgive them, for they do not know what they are doing." Luke 23:34 NIV

FREED BY FORGIVENESS

Daily we are offered opportunities to participate in the miracle of forgiveness and the new life it brings. A husband or wife is unkind, forgets a request, or thoughtlessly hurts our feelings. We can choose to bear a grudge or to forgive. A friend repeats gossip about us, takes credit for something we accomplished, or rebuffs us. We can devise ways to get even or release our hurt through the act of forgiving. A child rejects our advice or makes a choice of which we disapprove. We can decide to offer condemnation or to offer forgiveness.

"But they don't even ask for forgiveness!" "They don't even seem sorry!" we might respond. But when we look at Jesus on the cross, we see that forgiveness is not based on the behavior of the one committing the offense, but rather upon the character of the one who forgives. What a revelation for many of us! We have the power to forgive regardless of what another person chooses to think or do. By forgiving we do not absolve the other person of responsibility, we simply refuse to carry the burden of anger, hatred, or bitterness around any longer. We are freed from the bondage of negative and destructive emotions as well as from the temptation to indulge in bad behavior by getting even or striking back.

At the cross, Jesus demonstrated the cost of God's forgiveness. It required His death. But three days later, He also demonstrated the power of such forgiveness: the freedom of resurrection and new life. Why should we practice this Easter kind of forgiveness? I believe the key is found several places in the Scripture, but perhaps it is stated most clearly in the two verses immediately following what we refer to as The Lord's Prayer: "For if you forgive men when they sin against you, your heavenly Father will also forgive you. But if you do not forgive men their sins, your Father will not forgive your sins" (Matthew 6:14, 15 NIV). Our ability to receive God's forgiveness is inextricably bound up in our own willingness to extend it to others. If we harbor an unforgiving spirit, we only hurt ourselves.

Forgiveness is not a sign of weakness, but of strength. It makes us partners in the great compassion that God extended to mankind at Calvary two thousand years ago. If Jesus could look upon those who brutalized and berated Him and offer them forgiveness, can we do less to those who hurt us? Forgiveness is an opportunity to experience the freeing power of the Resurrection every day. It is often difficult, but we can take comfort in the knowledge that God does not ask us to do anything He does not empower us to accomplish.

> *Father, I know that You forgive me, but I acknowledge that it is often difficult for me to extend that same forgiveness to others. Free me from my feelings of anger and bitterness through the choice to forgive, so that I may experience a resurrection lifestyle all year long.*

Two friends share their thoughts in PEASANT WOMEN SEATED, CHATTING *by French artist Causant Paysannes Assisses. Image from Christie's Images/Superstock.*

On an Easter Morn

Jessie Cannon Eldridge

Let me think deeply when the Easter comes,
Look to my soul and weigh its faith and hope,
Rededicate it; then lead those who grope
In unbelief into the light that sums
Our living up in such a wondrous way;
Show them the meaning of the Easter songs,
The lily flowers, the gathering of the throngs,
The hallelujahs; teach them how to pray.
We should be happy on an Easter morn,
Rejoicing with Christ's glorious rebirth,
Joining to spread His message around the earth,
And beckoning others to again be born.

Call all who wander, who have sinned, known loss,
"Come, rise again, and conquer o'er the cross!"

Easter Offering

Helen Gee Woods

I fashion you these lilies, orchids too;
In crystal vases here they stand en masse,
Enriching velvet petals lift anew
As morning sunlight sparkles through the grass.
The voices thrill in praise of Easter-song,
Illuminate the dawn in pageantry.
"The Christ is risen" heralds through the throng
While whispers stir to immortality.
New birth is hailed with victory to esteem.
With senses clarified we kneel to pray
That from this resurrected morn, redeem
The vision that would guide us on our way.

Oh, may our freedom from the grave be borne,
An offering for Christ this Easter morn.

A gift of lilies is a gift of spring. Photo by Gene Ahrens.

The Triumphant Entry

And it came to pass, when he was come nigh to Bethphage and Bethany, at the mount called the mount of Olives, he sent two of his disciples, Saying, Go ye into the village over against you; in the which at your entering ye shall find a colt tied, whereon yet never man sat: loose him, and bring him hither. And if any man ask you, Why do ye loose him? thus shall ye say unto him, Because the Lord hath need of him.

And they that were sent went their way, and found even as he had said unto them. And as they were loosing the colt, the owners thereof said unto them, Why loose ye the colt? And they said, The Lord hath need of him.

And they brought him to Jesus: and they cast their garments upon the colt, and they set Jesus thereon. And as he went, they spread their clothes in the way. And when he was come nigh, even now at the descent of the mount of Olives, the whole multitude of the disciples began to rejoice and praise God with a loud voice for all the mighty works that they had seen; Saying, Blessed be the King that cometh in the name of the Lord: peace in heaven, and glory in the highest.

Luke 19:29–38

Christ is greeted with praise and palm branches in ENTRY OF CHRIST INTO JERUSALEM *by artist Pietro Lorenzetti (c. 1280–1348).* Image from San Franscesco, Assisi/ET Archive, London/Superstock.

Jesus Washes the Disciples' Feet

Now before the feast of the passover, when Jesus knew that his hour was come that he should depart out of this world unto the Father, having loved his own which were in the world, he loved them unto the end.

And supper being ended, the devil having now put into the heart of Judas Iscariot, Simon's son, to betray him; Jesus knowing that the Father had given all things into his hands, and that he was come from God, and went to God; He riseth from supper, and laid aside his garments; and took a towel, and girded himself. After that he poureth water into a basin, and began to wash the disciples' feet, and to wipe them with the towel wherewith he was girded.

Then cometh he to Simon Peter: and Peter saith unto him, Lord, dost thou wash my feet? Jesus answered and said unto him, What I do thou knowest not now; but thou shalt know hereafter. Peter saith unto him, Thou shalt never wash my feet. Jesus answered him, If I wash thee not, thou hast no part with me. Simon Peter saith unto him, Lord, not my feet only, but also my hands and my head.

So after he had washed their feet, and had taken his garments, and was set down again, he said unto them, Know ye what I have done to you? Ye call me Master and Lord: and ye say well; for so I am. If I then, your Lord and Master, have washed your feet; ye also ought to wash one another's feet. For I have given you an example, that ye should do as I have done to you.

Verily, verily, I say unto you, The servant is not greater than his lord; neither he that is sent greater than he that sent him. If ye know these things, happy are ye if ye do them. I speak not of you all: I know whom I have chosen: but that the scripture may be fulfilled, He that eateth bread with me hath lifted up his heel against me. Now I tell you before it come, that, when it is come to pass, ye may believe that I am he. Verily, verily, I say unto you, He that receiveth whomsoever I send receiveth me; and he that receiveth me receiveth him that sent me.

John 13:1–9, 12–20

Jesus demonstrates true humility in The Washing of the Feet *by artist Pietro Lorenzetti (c. 1280–1348). Image from S. Franscesco, Assisi, Italy/Scala/Art Resource, New York.*

Jesus before the High Priest

And the chief priests and all the council sought for witness against Jesus to put him to death; and found none. For many bare false witness against him, but their witness agreed not together. And there arose certain, and bare false witness against him, saying, We heard him say, I will destroy this temple that is made with hands, and within three days I will build another made without hands. But neither so did their witness agree together.

And the high priest stood up in the midst, and asked Jesus, saying, Answerest thou nothing? what is it which these witness against thee? But he held his peace, and answered nothing. Again the high priest asked him, and said unto him, Art thou the Christ, the Son of the Blessed?

And Jesus said, I am: and ye shall see the Son of man sitting on the right hand of power, and coming in the clouds of heaven. Then the high priest rent his clothes, and saith, What need we any further witnesses? Ye have heard the blasphemy: what think ye? And they all condemned him to be guilty of death.

And some began to spit on him, and to cover his face, and to buffet him, and to say unto him, Prophesy: and the servants did strike him with the palms of their hands.

Mark 14:55–65

Christ faces his accusers in FLAGELLATION OF CHRIST *by artist Pietro Lorenzetti (c. 1280–1348). Image from S. Franscesco, Assisi, Italy/Scala/Art Resource, New York.*

The Way of the Cross

Then came Jesus forth, wearing the crown of thorns, and the purple robe. And Pilate saith unto them, Behold the man! When the chief priests therefore and officers saw him, they cried out, saying, Crucify him, crucify him. Pilate saith unto them, Take ye him, and crucify him: for I find no fault in him. The Jews answered him, We have a law, and by our law he ought to die, because he made himself the Son of God. When Pilate therefore heard that saying, he was the more afraid; And went again into the judgment hall, and saith unto Jesus, Whence art thou? But Jesus gave him no answer.

Then saith Pilate unto him, Speakest thou not unto me? knowest thou not that I have power to crucify thee, and have power to release thee? Jesus answered, Thou couldest have no power at all against me, except it were given thee from above: therefore he that delivered me unto thee hath the greater sin. And from thenceforth Pilate sought to release him: but the Jews cried out, saying, If thou let this man go, thou art not Caesar's friend: whosoever maketh himself a king speaketh against Caesar. When Pilate therefore heard that saying, he brought Jesus forth, and sat down in the judgment seat in a place that is called the Pavement, but in the Hebrew, Gabbatha.

Then delivered he him therefore unto them to be crucified. And they took Jesus, and led him away. And he bearing his cross went forth into a place called the place of a skull, which is called in the Hebrew Golgotha: Where they crucified him, and two other with him, on either side one, and Jesus in the midst.

John 19:5–13, 16–18

Artist Pietro Lorenzetti (c. 1280–1348) depicts Jesus struggling under the weight of the cross in WAY TO CALVARY. *Image from S. Franscesco, Assisi, Italy/Scala/Art Resource, New York.*

The Resurrection

In the end of the sabbath, as it began to dawn toward the first day of the week, came Mary Magdalene and the other Mary to see the sepulchre. And, behold, there was a great earthquake: for the angel of the Lord descended from heaven, and came and rolled back the stone from the door, and sat upon it. His countenance was like lightning, and his raiment white as snow: And for fear of him the keepers did shake, and became as dead men.

And the angel answered and said unto the women, Fear not ye: for I know that ye seek Jesus, which was crucified. He is not here: for he is risen, as he said. Come, see the place where the Lord lay. And go quickly, and tell his disciples that he is risen from the dead; and, behold, he goeth before you into Galilee; there shall ye see him: lo, I have told you.

And they departed quickly from the sepulchre with fear and great joy; and did run to bring his disciples word.

And as they went to tell his disciples, behold, Jesus met them, saying, All hail. And they came and held him by the feet, and worshipped him. Then said Jesus unto them, Be not afraid: go tell my brethren that they go into Galilee, and there shall they see me.

Then the eleven disciples went away into Galilee, into a mountain where Jesus had appointed them. And when they saw him, they worshipped him: but some doubted.

And Jesus came and spake unto them, saying, All power is given unto me in heaven and in earth. Go ye therefore, and teach all nations, baptizing them in the name of the Father, and of the Son, and of the Holy Ghost: Teaching them to observe all things whatsoever I have commanded you: and, lo, I am with you always, even unto the end of the world. Amen.

Matthew 28:1–10, 16–20

Jesus rises from the tomb in RESURRECTION OF CHRIST *by artist Pietro Lorenzetti (c. 1280–1348).*
Image from S. Franscesco, Assisi, Italy/Scala/Art Resource, New York.

A Ballad of Trees and the Master

Sidney Lanier

Into the woods my Master went,
Clean forspent, forspent.
Into the woods, my Master came,
Forspent with love and shame,
But the olives they were not blind to Him,
The little gray leaves were kind to Him:
The thorn-tree had a mind to Him
When into the woods He came.

Out of the woods my Master went,
And He was well content.
Out of the woods my Master came,
Content with death and shame.
When Death and Shame would woo Him last,
From under the trees they drew Him last:
'Twas on a tree they slew Him—last
When out of the woods He came.

*Morning sun peeks through an aspen grove in Colorado's
Gunnison National Forest. Photo by Steve Terrill.*

THROUGH MY WINDOW

Pamela Kennedy

Art by Pat Thompson

EMMAUS MIRACLE

I tell you, Cleopas, it's all wishful thinking," said the shorter man, shaking his head at his companion while they plodded down the road to Emmaus. "Do you actually believe what they said? You were there. You saw Him hanging on the cross. Don't you remember how Joseph and Nicodemus took Jesus' body and placed it in the tomb?"

"I know, I know." Cleopas raised his hand to stop his friend. "Of course I was there. I saw exactly what you did, but the women say that this very morning, before the sun rose, they actually spoke with Jesus. What do you make of that?"

"Hysterics! They see what they want to see. They

also spoke of angels in white robes. Do you believe that too?"

Cleopas hesitated, then raised his face to the sky. He sighed. "I don't know what to believe. I followed Jesus for almost three years thinking He would bring us the kingdom of God, and things are worse than before. I believed Him when He said He was the Messiah, and now He's dead. Everything I trusted seems to have failed. I no longer know what is true and what is only a dream, my friend."

From the corner of his eye, Cleopas detected movement, stopped, and turned. A man in a dusty cloak approached him and smiled. "Good day," he said. "You two seem to be deep in conversation. What is it that so occupies you as you walk?"

Cleopas looked at the man with disdain. "You must be the only person in Jerusalem who doesn't know what has just happened there!"

"I don't know what you're talking about." The man shaded his eyes in the late afternoon sun and continued, "Tell me what you mean."

Cleopas placed his hand on the man's shoulder and spoke as if to a very young child or someone dull of understanding. "We speak of Jesus from Nazareth, whom many of us believed was the prophet, come to establish God's kingdom. He traveled throughout Judea teaching, performing miracles, healing, even raising the dead. But our religious leaders determined He was a dangerous heretic and convinced the authorities to sentence Him to death. That was three days ago. Today, some women we know came to us with tales of angels and a mysteriously opened tomb and an empty grave. Two of our friends went and found the tomb as the women had said, but they didn't see Jesus. So we are all faced with this perplexing puzzle: was He the Messiah or wasn't He, is He dead or isn't He? That is what we are talking about." He turned to his companion, pointed down the road, and walked away from the stranger.

"You aren't as perceptive as you think," the stranger called out as he caught up with the two surprised men and matched his pace to theirs. Before they could object, he continued. "You obviously know the Scriptures. You should believe what they say. Did Isaiah not prophesy that the Christ would suffer before he entered his glory?"

The man gestured with animation, weaving a tapestry with his words as the three of them continued down the road. "Remember when Moses led the children of Israel out of the bondage of Egypt. . ." His voice wafted on the breeze behind the trio as their heads bent together and their feet marked off the miles to Emmaus.

Cleopas stopped suddenly, startled to see the familiar surroundings of his home so soon. Where had the time gone? The stranger lifted his cloak about his shoulders and head, said, "Shalom," then turned to continue on his way.

"Wait!" Cleopas's voice echoed with urgency in the early evening. "You have walked a long way with us, perhaps you would stay a while so we could share a meal together. My house is very near." Cleopas was not really so hungry for food as he was for more of the stranger's words, for they nourished the emptiness in his heart. When the man hesitated, Cleopas entreated once more. "Please stay awhile. It is late."

"I will stay just a little longer," he said quietly, a smile curving the edges of his mouth.

They entered Cleopas's house, and he had bread, cheese, and fruit quickly brought to the table. Without hesitation, the stranger reached for the flat wheat loaf, lifted it, and offered thanks to God. Then he broke the bread and offered it to the two men.

Cleopas felt his heart leap. He couldn't tear his eyes from the stranger's, for they were no longer those of an unknown traveling companion. His mind fought to grasp the impossible truth as he raised his trembling hand to take the broken bread, and when his fingers brushed those of his risen Lord, he whispered, "Jesus." In that instant, Christ disappeared.

The two men stared at the crumbs upon the table and the place where their Master had been. Cleopas clasped the bread to his chest as if it were precious gold. "Didn't you feel a burning in your heart when He spoke to us of the prophets and the Messiah as we walked?" he whispered.

"Indeed, and when He explained the Scriptures I could understand the meaning of them all! It was as if He removed the blindness from my soul! We must run and tell the others that Christ lives and has revealed Himself to us!"

The two men jumped up from the table and hurriedly gathered their cloaks and two oil lamps to light their way. They raced from the house, disregarding the darkness of the Judean night, for they carried more than the light of two small lamps as they ran to join the other disciples. In their hearts they carried the bright assurance of the resurrection that would shine through the ages with the message of eternal life for all believers: The kingdom *is* come! God's will *has been* done! The Saviour lives and reigns!

Pamela Kennedy is a freelance writer of short stories, articles, essays, and children's books. Wife of a retired naval officer and mother of three children, she has made her home on both U.S. coasts and currently resides in Honolulu, Hawaii.

Ring, Happy Bells

Lucy Larcom

Ring, happy bells of Eastertime!
The world is glad to hear your chime;
Across wide fields of melting snow
The winds of summer softly blow,
And birds and streams repeat the chime
Of Eastertime.

Ring, happy bells of Eastertime!
The world takes up your chant sublime,
"The Lord is risen!" The night of fear
Has passed away, and heaven draws near:
We breathe the air of that blest clime,
At Eastertime.

Ring, happy bells of Eastertime!
Our happy hearts give back your chime!
The Lord is risen! We die no more:
He opens wide the heavenly door;
He meets us, while to Him we climb,
At Eastertime.

Azaleas and Spanish moss frame a church on St. Simon's Island in Georgia. Photo by William Johnson/Johnson's Photography.

Bells of
St. Michael

Mary Weston Fordham

On the gladsome Easter morning,
When the earliest flow'rets bloom,
Snowdrops pure and violets purple
Blend to scatter sweet perfume;
Then your happiest notes are
    poured forth,
Then your jubilee is heard
Pealing out in joyful accents,
Chiming, "God is very good."

From that ancient lofty turret,
O'erlooking land and sea,
Peals of comfort have been wafted,
Sounds of gladness o'er the lea.
Many a storm-tossed, weary wanderer
Looked to thee as hope's bright star,
Listened to thy mellow chiming,
Smiling as he crossed the bar.

Dear old bells, your music thrills me,
Whether rung in joy or woe,
They recall the joyous springtime
Of fond mem'ry's long ago.
Sweetly chime through all the ages;
As time's cycles swiftly move;
Peal forth loudly, God is gracious;
Whisper softly, He is love.

Easter Day

Harold A. Schulz

On that first glorious Easter day the dawn
Must have contained some unused color tones
To brighten up the sky with dusty rose
Followed with countless hues of reds and gold.

The air that life was giv'n to breathe must have
Vibrated with the energy of love.
The lilies by the way were trumpets which
Declared the splendor of the thrilling morn.

The rose of sharon and varieties
Of wild flowers graced the peaceful countryside.
From somewhere o'er a hill an ear could catch
The anxious bleating of a newborn lamb.

And from each tree, blessed with a nest of birds
There came from newly broken shells a song
Giving a message of good cheer and joy,
A melody the world had never heard.

These are the things that spring's glad Easter gives
Today as dawn comes bright and full and new.

A young pet lamb. Photo by Superstock.
A row of oaks line Hamms Lake in Washington. Photo by Steve Terrill.

There Is No Unbelief

Elizabeth York Case

There is no unbelief:
Whoever plants a seed beneath the sod
And waits to see it push away the clod—
　　He trusts in God.

There is no unbelief:
Whoever says beneath the sky,
"Be patient, heart; light breaketh by and by,"
　　Trusts the Most High.

There is no unbelief:
Whoever sees 'neath winter's field of snow
The silent harvests of the future grow—
　　God's power must know.

There is no unbelief:
Whoever lies down on his couch to sleep,
Content to lock each sense in slumber deep,
　　Knows God will keep.

There is no unbelief:
Whoever says "tomorrow," "the unknown,"
"The future," trusts that power alone
　　He dares disown.

There is no unbelief:
The heart that looks on when the eyelids close
And dares to live when life has only woes,
　　God's comfort knows.

There is no unbelief:
For this by day and night unconsciously
The heart lives by the faith the lips deny.
　　God knoweth why.

A young girl takes time to smell the flowers in Mt. Vernon, Washington. Photo by Jim Cummins/FPG International.

Joyous Spring

Harriet Feltham

There's growth in the ground this morning,
For the fields have been planted to grain,
And it lifts its eyes
To the dreary skies
And drinks in the soft spring rain.

There's warmth in the air this morning,
For the frost has left the earth,
And the budding trees
And the honey bees
Are restored with a fresh new birth.

The river is singing this morning
As it ripples around the quay,
And its merry song
As it flows along
Makes the world seem vibrant and gay.

There's joy all around this morning,
With the vital breath of spring,
An urge to toil
In the fertile soil,
To labor, to love, to sing.

from A Land That Man Has Newly Trod

Joaquin Miller

A land that man has newly trod,
A land that only God has known,
Through all the soundless cycles flown.
Yet perfect blossoms bless the sod,
And perfect birds illume the trees,
And perfect unheard harmonies
Pour out eternally to God.

*Rows of corn march across a hill in Craftsbury, Vermont.
Photo by William Johnson/Johnson's Photography.*

BEAUTY IS LONG IN BUILDING

Amy Bower

It takes a winter to create a spring.
The daffodils and jonquils, buried deep,
Are not, as they may seem, in idle sleep.
They are the actors waiting in a wing
And touching up their makeup coloring.
The barren branches of the peach tree leap
Against the wind, rehearsing so to keep
The dancing feet of June in perfect swing.

Then when the stage is set, the curtains part,
The buckeye shows her rosy candle flame
And softly lovely pastorals are sung,
Released and stirred by magic, hidden art.
Beauty is long in building—it became
The treasury of God when years were young.

Beauty is God's handwriting—a wayside sacrament. Welcome it in every fair face, in every fair sky, in every fair flower, and thank God for it as a cup of blessing.

—Ralph Waldo Emerson

Wildflowers cascade over the edge of a small stream in Colorado's Uncompahgre National Forest. Photo by Dennis Frates/Oregon Scenics.

TRAVELER'S Diary

REDWOOD NATIONAL FOREST

Noel Shriver

After a lifetime as a New Englander, I am discovering the American West Coast. Relocating from Boston to coastal Washington three years ago has meant more than a change in address. It has meant a complete change in perspective. I first felt it on the flight across country. Soaring over the mountains of the northwest left me completely in awe. We have beautiful mountains in New England, but even the more rugged White Mountains of New Hampshire seem like rolling hills as I flew over the Rockies and the Cascades. The West is simply bigger than the East, and looking at the rugged landscape below, I began to understand why so many people hold this image of New England as a collection of quaint villages. This spring on my first trip to Redwood National Forest, I discovered something else that is bigger in the west: the trees. Inside this national park, the trees seem to have grown in size to match their mountain neighbors.

When Friar Juan Crespi, the man who gave the redwoods their name, first came upon California's forest of giant trees in 1769, it covered over two million acres. By 1965, logging had reduced the forest to 300,000 acres. In 1968, Congress and the state of California cooperated to protect the redwoods, and the national park was established to protect one of our most beloved national treasures.

My visit to Redwood National Forest coincided with the blooming of the park's rhododendrons. But as beautiful as these blossoms were, they were no match for the park's stars, the giant redwood and sequoia trees. Coast redwoods can live up to two thousand years, although they average five to seven hundred years of age. The tallest redwood is almost four hundred feet. These trees grow from the size of a tomato seed to a weight of five hundred tons—not quite the stately old maples I am used to from home.

My tour began on US Route 101, also known as the Redwood Highway. My first stop was the Lady Bird Johnson Grove, named for the former first lady who devoted much of her energy to beautifying our natural landscape. The grove features a mile-long trail through the forest. Along the quiet, dark trail, I saw giant hollowed-out trees still standing. Park rangers told me they were called "goose trees" and had been used by early settlers to shelter livestock.

A few miles further up 101, I stopped to see the aptly named "Big Tree." Standing alone, this redwood rises to 304 feet, is twenty-one feet in diameter and sixty-six feet in circumference. It is estimated to be fifteen hundred years old. Words cannot really describe the wonder of these trees. I can record how tall they are, how old they are, how thick they are, but until you have stood before a giant redwood or sequoia, their immensity is impossible to fathom.

I ended my visit on the Coastal Trail. The walk begins at Klamath Overlook, which provides a breathtaking view of the rugged coastline, and the chance, although I was not so lucky, to see gray whales swimming by. The trail winds for four miles along the coast and gives an up-close view of the diverse natural life of this spectacular park.

The image of the giant redwood trees is familiar to every American, but one must really visit the park to grasp their true grandeur. These trees offer a perfect symbol for my feelings about west- versus east-coast America. Being away from the familiar, from friends and family, is never easy. But the most spectacular discovery I have made since my relocation—these marvelous giant trees—confirms what I saw looking out the window of my airplane. Things grow bigger here. Not that one is better or worse, but it is, to this New Englander, truly awe-inspiring.

Rhododendrons bloom amid the undergrowth in California's Redwood National Park. Photo by D. Muench/H. Armstrong Roberts.

TREE PLANTING

Samuel F. Smith

Joy for the sturdy trees,
Fanned by each fragrant breeze,
　　Lovely they stand.
The song-birds o'er them trill;
They shade each tinkling rill;
They crown each swelling hill,
　　Lowly or grand.

Plant them by stream and way;
Plant them where children play
　　And toilers rest,
In every verdant vale,
On every sunny swale,
Whether to grow or fail;
　　God knoweth best.

Select the strong, the fair;
Plant them with earnest care,
　　No toil is vain.
Plant in a fitter place,
Where, like a lovely face
Set in some sweeter grace,
　　Change may prove gain.

God will His blessing send;
All things on Him depend.
　　His loving care
Clings to each leaf and flower
Like ivy to its tower;
His presence and His power
　　Are everywhere.

Blooming magnolia trees form a tunnel of blooms.
Photo by Superstock.

LEGENDARY AMERICANS

J. STERLING MORTON

Like countless other nineteenth-century Americans, J. Sterling Morton joined the great westward movement that, like a tidal wave, expanded our nation from the Atlantic Ocean to the Pacific Coast. He caught the swell in Detroit, Michigan, and with his wife, rode it to the Great Plains of the Nebraska territory where, in 1854, he prepared to set down new roots. Like his fellow pioneers, Morton was awed by the western landscape. The enormous, wide-open, uninhabited spaces were both thrilling and frightening to eyes accustomed to the already tamed eastern country. Whereas most of his new neighbors looked out upon the vast, treeless plains of Nebraska territory and wondered how they would tame the alien landscape to meet their needs, Morton thought more in terms of forming a partner-

ship with the land than of conquering it. Settlers were coming, Morton knew by the thousands, by the millions. Nebraska would not long remain wild and untouched. The settlers would transform the landscape with their homes, towns, and farms. If they were to prosper, if the land were to flourish, Morton knew, that transformation must be made with care and planning. The Nebraska pioneers, Morton decided, must plant trees.

Sterling Morton had always loved trees. But he was neither a farmer nor a botanist by trade; he was a journalist. And it was with a journalist's skills that Morton set about his crusade to bring trees to the plains of the Nebraska territory. Within a few years of his arrival in the West, Morton had become the editor of Nebraska's first newspaper, and the pages of this paper became his forum for spreading the word about trees.

Morton's readers were not a hard sell. Mostly Easterners by birth, they missed the trees they had grown up taking for granted. But Morton knew that the issue was more than an emotional or aesthetic one. Nebraska needed trees, he repeated time and time again in his editorials, not just to make the settlers feel at home and to please the eye, but to anchor the soil, to provide wood for their fireplaces, to produce lumber for building their homes, and to shade them from the scorching summer sun. Morton called upon every Nebraskan to plant a tree. He urged churches and schools and towns and every other organized group in the territory to plant trees. He made the act of planting a tree a civic duty for each and every citizen.

Nebraskans heeded Morton's advice. As he rose in status to the position of secretary of the Nebraska territory, trees rose up across the plains. In 1872, Morton proposed an official day for tree planting. The government of the territory agreed; and on April 10, 1872, Nebraska celebrated its first Arbor Day with the planting of more than one million trees. The holiday was emphasized especially in the territorial schools, where the youngest Nebraskans, many first generation native-born Westerners, learned about the vital importance of trees to the landscape and about their own responsibility to care for the land upon which they lived.

In a speech on that first Arbor Day, Morton painted a broad picture of the importance of trees and plants to human life. He spoke of the countless practical uses of trees in man's everyday life: building materials, fuel, shade. He talked of the beauty of trees, how they added color and grace to the landscape. And he also spoke of the need for each generation of mankind to guard the earth as a sacred trust. "Each generation takes the earth as trustees," Morton said, "We ought to bequeath to posterity as many forests and orchards as we have exhausted and consumed." Morton stressed the place of trees in the great cycle of life on earth. He spoke of how trees cleaned the air, fed and housed the animals, and how, in death, their decay enriched the soil and nurtured new growth. No one who heard Morton speak that day could ever again take the presence of trees for granted.

Sterling Morton's Arbor Day was a great public success; and like the branches of the trees that were growing throughout the territory, the holiday spread. In 1882, Arbor Day became a nationwide celebration. More than one hundred years later, Arbor Day is observed with tree planting and educational programs in every American state.

It is instructive to remember that in Morton's day most of America was not treeless like the Nebraska plains. In the East, American settlers had struggled for generations to clear the great forests that covered the land; working with the illusion of infinite abundance, they had grown into the habit of consumption and destruction. But Morton's foresight was as important to these Americans as it was to those on the Great Plains. For what Sterling Morton taught was that no human civilization could live without trees— and that they must plant them where they lacked them, certainly, but just as importantly, they must safeguard them even where they seemed to proliferate. Morton was among the earliest group of Americans to look into the future and see that if America continued on its present course, a time would come when the forests would all be cleared and consumed. His Arbor Day helped Americans stem the tide of depletion and to start thinking of what kind of landscape they would leave for their grandchildren.

Certainly Morton's message has not been heeded in every corner. Our forests are still being cut down, and our landscape is frequently ravaged by thoughtless development. But the battle he helped begin has been joined; today, groups exist in every corner of America to protect and enhance our trees and other natural resources. And every spring on Arbor Day, schools, churches, civic groups, families, and individuals still plant trees, each of them a tribute to the vision of Sterling Morton, who saw himself as a steward, not a master, of the magnificent American landscape and urged every citizen to do the same.

Nancy Skarmeas is a book editor and mother of a toddler, Gordon, who is keeping her and her husband quite busy at their home in New Hampshire. Her Greek and Irish ancestry has fostered a lifelong interest in research and history.

OUR HERITAGE

ARBOR DAY LETTER TO SCHOOLCHILDREN OF THE UNITED STATES, 1907
PRESIDENT THEODORE ROOSEVELT

Arbor Day, which simply means "Tree Day," is now observed in every state in our Union—and mainly in the schools. At various times, from January to December, but chiefly in this month of April, you give a day or part of a day to special exercises and perhaps to actual tree planting, in recognition of the importance of trees as a Nation, and of what they yield in adornment, comfort, and useful products to the communities in which you live.

It is well that you should celebrate your Arbor Day thoughtfully, for within your lifetime the Nation's need of trees will become serious. We of an older generation can get along with what we have, though with growing hardship; but in your full manhood and womanhood you will want what nature once so bountifully supplied, and man so thoughtlessly destroyed; and because of that want you will reproach us, not for what we have used, but for what we have wasted.

For the nation, as for the man or woman or boy or girl, the road to success is the right use of what we have and the improvement of present opportunity. . . . A people without children would face a hopeless future; a country without trees is almost as hopeless; forests which are so used that they cannot renew themselves will soon vanish, and with them all their benefits. A true forest is not merely a storehouse full of wood, but, as it were, a factory of wood, and at the same time a reservoir of water. When you help to preserve our forests or plant new ones you are acting the part of good citizens. The value of forestry deserves, therefore, to be taught in the schools, which aim to make good citizens of you. If your Arbor Day exercises help you to realize what benefits each one of you receives from the forests, and how by your assistance these benefits may continue, they will serve a good end.

ABOUT THE TEXT

By 1882, Americans nationwide observed Arbor Day, and nowhere was the holiday more openly embraced than in the schoolroom. Individual classes or grades gathered every April to plant a tree, label it, and learn how to care for it. Parades, songs, and the recitation of Arbor Day poetry added to the festivities. President Theodore Roosevelt wrote the above letter in 1907 and applauded these efforts to teach children the importance of America's trees and wise environmental stewardship.

A flowering dogwood creates a lovely focal point in this northern Illinois garden. Photo by Jessie Walker.

Feathered Friend

Kay Hoffman

Welcome back, my feathered friend,
I'm glad to see you're here.
All winter long I have missed
Your morning songs of cheer.

Anxiously I've watched for you,
My special springtime boarder;
I hope that you'll be pleased to see
Your birdhouse is in order.

You'll find your bill is paid in full,
Small payment for a tune.
The feeder's filled with choicest seeds;
In bird bath you may groom.

For you, my pretty feathered friend,
I've penned this little poem.
I hope that you'll enjoy your stay;
Please make yourself at home.

*Cherry blossoms fill a portion of sky in Multnomah County,
Oregon. Photo by Steve Terrill.*

Spring

Mary Borrelli

A sunbeam swept into the room,
Chasing cobwebs of March gloom,
While outside in the flower bed
A crocus raised her sleepy head.
A feathered chorus bade us sing
To praise the miracle of spring.

My Special Thanks

Beverly J. Anderson

The birds have found my cherry tree.
Their songs are sheer delight;
They flutter mid the greening leaves
And blossoms snowy white.

Each year my feathered friends return
And claim my cherry tree.
This lovely sight and musicale
Awakens spring in me.

Their happy tunes proclaim that spring
Has come to bless the earth,
And I join in with joyful praise
For spring's gift of rebirth.

Oh, thank You, God, for singing birds
And lacy cherry trees
That give a weary heart new hope—
My special thanks for these.

HANDMADE HEIRLOOM

A unique family tree, complemented by artist Eve DeGrie's original watercolor, reflects four generations of editor Michelle Burke's family.

FAMILY TREE

Nancy Skarmeas

I have a friend who has created a remarkable family tree chart. Framed on his living room wall, this record bears no resemblance at all to a tree. Instead, it is a fan-shaped diagram that has the look of an architectural drawing. My friend placed his own name in the bottom center of the fan and then, moving out in succeeding half circles, he added the names of his parents, his grandparents, and so on through thirteen generations. The lines of the fan were precisely drawn; the names were carefully hand-lettered in black ink. The result is beautiful and impressive. Looking upon his work, I was inspired by the idea of the family tree as a work of art, as something not just to file in a safe-deposit box or a folder, but to hang on the wall as an object of beauty and history.

Creating a family tree is an idea that has universal appeal. But it is also a project that can seem very daunting. When I think of family trees, I tend to think of charts such as my friend's that trace an individual's roots back through several generations. But like so many American families, mine is not well-documented. My ancestors moved from one country to another and mostly left their past behind. But this year, inspired by my friend's creation and prompted by the passage of time and the desire to create a unique gift for my mother, I decided to put aside my fears. I will become my family's historian and put together a family tree that will become a treasured heirloom.

The first step in any family history project is information gathering. Family information comes from a variety of sources. Start with family members themselves. Ask questions of your family's eldest members. Write down any names, dates, and places they can provide. I began with my own mother and her store-house of memories. She in turn contacted her siblings and their children and began to record marriages, births, and deaths. Other possible sources are paper records in family albums, scrapbooks, and Bibles. Public records can be of help to some searchers, but offer nothing at all for others. It all depends upon where and when your ancestors lived. Each search will be as unique as the particular family.

When I had accumulated a notebook full of information, I sat and looked at the names before me. If I envisioned a traditional family tree, one that traced back a single line through parents and grandparents, I had only myself, my parents, and their parents to fill the branches. Approached from this angle, I was left with a small list for a family that is by all measures unusually large. That is when I began to think creatively. My friend—he of the complete, thirteen-generation family fan—was the descendant of seventeenth-century New Englanders. His family had kept detailed personal records and were prominent in the public record. My family was a patchwork of recent immigrants. My grandparents had come here, taken on new names, and had cut their ties with the past in order to build a future. As I thought about the differences between our family histories, I realized that whereas my family couldn't document far back in time, we could certainly trace ourselves wide. My mother is one of thirteen children; as her child I am one of forty-two first cousins whose births spanned nearly forty years. Thinking about these numbers, I began to envision the design for my family tree. Instead of tracing my own roots back, I would trace the descendants of my mother's parents forward through the years.

I am still in the gathering and planning stage. While I wait for the last names and dates to come in—including two or three recent births—I have begun sketching out a design. I have decided to display my own family information in the traditional form of a tree, but with a twist. Using my best hand-lettering in ivory ink on green paper, I will begin with the names of my grandparents and then branch off their thirteen children. I will add the names of spouses below and then branch their children off above them. My tree will grow outward toward the future. On its furthest reaching branches,

it will include five generations, but it will be the fullness of my tree that matters most. A family that would look small and sparse on a traditional tree chart will spread its branches wide on my tree design, for it will include not just parents and grandparents, but sisters and brothers, aunts and uncles, and first, second, and third cousins. Completed, it will be what we have always wanted, a record not of the distant past, but of the family that has grown here on American shores in the past one hundred years.

I have inspired others with my flexible approach to family trees. A friend has chosen to document her family with a display of photographs that reach back two generations and forward two. If photographs are available, this is a wonderful idea, sure to be a treasured keepsake. For her, the key to the project was the same as it was for me: she gathered the information and materials first and then decided upon a format that fit. After commissioning an artist to paint a watercolor tree on a large piece of matte board, my friend found a framer to cut holes in the board for photos of four generations of her family. Some families might proudly trace their roots back to a famous ancestor; others might cherish a long heritage in one particular city. A small, immediate family group is as worthy of celebrating as any other. No matter what the size or format, the project will be a success—regardless of its scope or shape—if it showcases what is important to you about your family.

At family gatherings, my mother often looks around at the extended group her family has become. We have all marveled at how so many people came about because of the union between her parents. This is what my family tree celebrates—my mother's pride in her own family and my grandparents' wonderful achievement of starting out alone in a new country and building a truly American family.

For me, creating a family tree has been an act of discovery. I guess I had always felt cheated at not being able to trace my family through the generations. Now I have discovered that a family tree is much more meaningful if it moves beyond a simple list of names and dates. If you find the right match between a family and a format, your family tree can become something truly unique. Every family has a story to tell; a little research and creative thought can turn your family's story into a one-of-a-kind heirloom.

I Shall Build a House

Sheila Stinson

I shall build a house at the foot of a hill
Near a silver stream that is cool and still.
I shall have a pine tree green and tall
And a weeping willow beside a wall.

A chimney of stone that is strong and wide
And a rambling rose to climb its side.
There will be a knocker upon the door
And a welcome mat on the porch's floor.

I shall make soft curtains, yellow and thin,
To help me entice the sunlight in.
I shall have a fireplace where logs will burn
And a pump outside and a butter churn.

Then, too, in my house there will be a place
Where children may wrestle and run and race.
I shall have a cat and a dog who'll be
The best of friends for my company.

One day I shall build this house of my dreams
Away from the world and its tiresome schemes.
Then I shall live at the foot of the hill
Near a silver stream that is cool and still.

*Artist Alfred William Parsons shares his version of a dream home
in* THE BOATHOUSE. *Image from Christie's Images.*

When Spring Comes

Jane W. Krows

When Mother takes the curtains down
And airs the bedding, say!
We know that winter's leaving us
And spring is on the way.

We scrub, we polish, dust and shine,
And not a spot escapes
Until the house is sanitized
From floors up to the drapes.

We find no time for loafing now,
No time for idle ways;
We eat a sandwich on the run
On Mom's spring cleaning days.

But, oh, how nice it all turns out—
The house, the trees, the weather—
All scrubbed so spotless every year
To welcome spring together.

A porch offers a cozy place to rest from a day of spring cleaning. Photo by Jessie Walker.

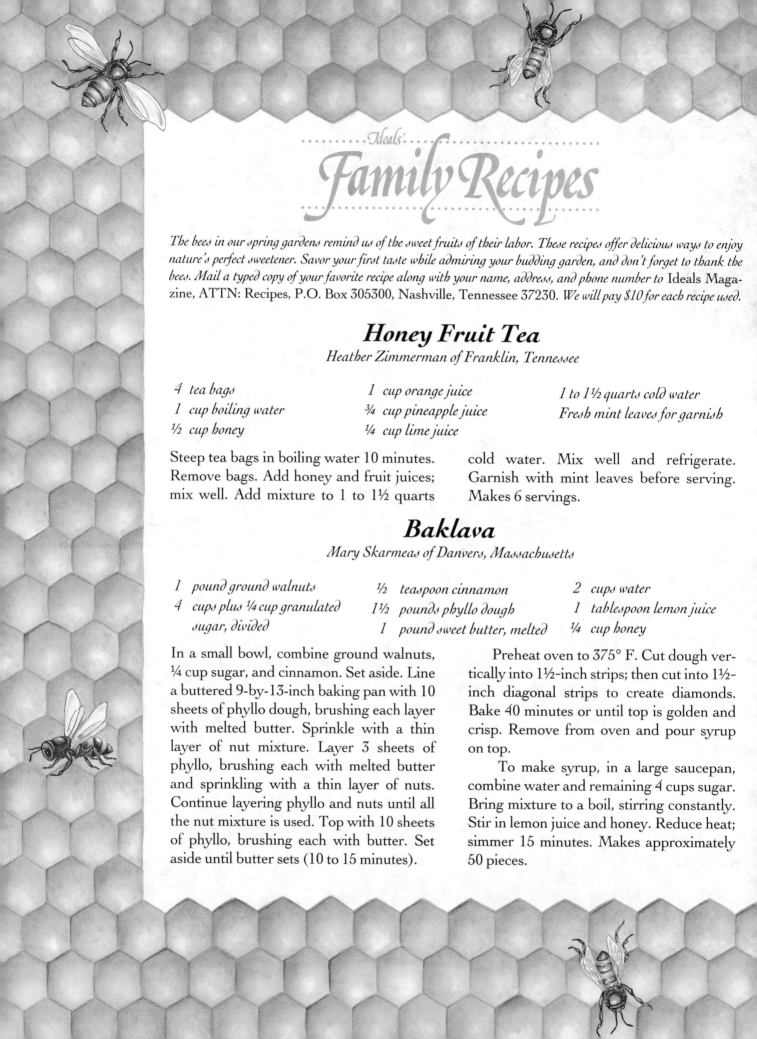

The bees in our spring gardens remind us of the sweet fruits of their labor. These recipes offer delicious ways to enjoy nature's perfect sweetener. Savor your first taste while admiring your budding garden, and don't forget to thank the bees. Mail a typed copy of your favorite recipe along with your name, address, and phone number to Ideals Magazine, ATTN: Recipes, P.O. Box 305300, Nashville, Tennessee 37230. *We will pay $10 for each recipe used.*

Honey Fruit Tea
Heather Zimmerman of Franklin, Tennessee

4 tea bags	1 cup orange juice	1 to 1½ quarts cold water
1 cup boiling water	¾ cup pineapple juice	Fresh mint leaves for garnish
½ cup honey	¼ cup lime juice	

Steep tea bags in boiling water 10 minutes. Remove bags. Add honey and fruit juices; mix well. Add mixture to 1 to 1½ quarts cold water. Mix well and refrigerate. Garnish with mint leaves before serving. Makes 6 servings.

Baklava
Mary Skarmeas of Danvers, Massachusetts

1 pound ground walnuts	½ teaspoon cinnamon	2 cups water
4 cups plus ¼ cup granulated sugar, divided	1½ pounds phyllo dough	1 tablespoon lemon juice
	1 pound sweet butter, melted	¼ cup honey

In a small bowl, combine ground walnuts, ¼ cup sugar, and cinnamon. Set aside. Line a buttered 9-by-13-inch baking pan with 10 sheets of phyllo dough, brushing each layer with melted butter. Sprinkle with a thin layer of nut mixture. Layer 3 sheets of phyllo, brushing each with melted butter and sprinkling with a thin layer of nuts. Continue layering phyllo and nuts until all the nut mixture is used. Top with 10 sheets of phyllo, brushing each with butter. Set aside until butter sets (10 to 15 minutes).

Preheat oven to 375° F. Cut dough vertically into 1½-inch strips; then cut into 1½-inch diagonal strips to create diamonds. Bake 40 minutes or until top is golden and crisp. Remove from oven and pour syrup on top.

To make syrup, in a large saucepan, combine water and remaining 4 cups sugar. Bring mixture to a boil, stirring constantly. Stir in lemon juice and honey. Reduce heat; simmer 15 minutes. Makes approximately 50 pieces.

Honey Lemon Squares

Evelyn Leatherman of Lancaster, England

½ cup butter, softened
¼ cup powdered sugar
1 cup plus 1 tablespoon flour, divided

¾ cup honey
½ cup lemon juice
3 eggs

1 teaspoon lemon zest
½ teaspoon baking powder

Preheat oven to 350° F. In a medium bowl, cream butter and powdered sugar until light and fluffy. Stir in flour. Press mixture evenly into the bottom of a 9-by-9-inch baking pan. Bake 20 minutes or until lightly browned.

Meanwhile, in a medium bowl, whisk together remaining 1 tablespoon flour with remaining ingredients until thoroughly blended. Pour mixture over baked crust. Bake an additional 20 to 25 minutes or until a knife inserted into the center comes out clean. Cool completely in pan before cutting into squares. Makes 12 servings.

Honey Fruit Truffles

Tamalyn Jackson of Miami Springs, Florida

6 ounces unsweetened chocolate, chopped
½ cup honey

2 tablespoons butter
2 tablespoons heavy cream

½ cup dried apricots, finely chopped
1 cup powdered sugar

In the top of a double boiler over gently boiling water, combine chocolate, honey, butter, and cream. Cook over medium heat, stirring constantly, until chocolate is melted and mixture is smooth. Stir in apricots. Refrigerate 1 hour or until mixture is firm. Roll rounded teaspoonfuls into balls. Roll each ball in powdered sugar. Makes 24 truffles.

Coconut Honey Cookies

Chloe Day of Mammoth Cave, Kentucky

2 tablespoons honey
¼ cup creamy peanut butter

¼ teaspoon salt
3 ounces semi-sweet chocolate

1 cup condensed milk
1½ cups shredded coconut

Preheat oven to 350° F. In a large bowl, combine honey, peanut butter, and salt. Set aside. In the top of a double boiler over boiling water, melt chocolate with condensed milk. Stir well. Pour chocolate mixture into the honey mixture. Stir in coconut. Drop by heaping teaspoonfuls 1 inch apart onto greased baking sheets. Bake 10 to 12 minutes. Remove to a wire rack to cool. Makes 2 dozen cookies.

BLUEBELLS OF NEW ENGLAND

Thomas Bailey Aldrich

The roses are a regal troop,
And modest folk the daisies;
But bluebells of New England,
To you I give my praises—

To you, fair phantoms in the sun,
Whom merry Spring discovers,
With bluebirds for your laureates
And honeybees for lovers.

The south-wind breathes,
    and lo! you throng
This rugged land of ours:
I think the pale blue clouds of May
Drop down and turn to flowers!

By cottage doors along the roads
You show your winsome faces,
And, like the spectre lady, haunt
The lonely woodland places.

All night your eyes are closed in sleep,
Kept fresh for day's adorning:
Such simple faith as yours can see
God's coming in the morning!

You lead me by your holiness
To pleasant ways of duty.
You set my thoughts to melody;
You fill me with your beauty.

Long may the heavens give you rain,
The sunshine its caresses;
Long may the woman that I love
Entwine you in her tresses!

A chorus of bluebells line a garden bed. Photo by Peter Gridley/FPG International.

Readers' Reflections

April
Diane L. Wright
Batavia, New York

April came to greet me
All clothed in springlike hues.
Flirtatious and capricious,
She drove away my blues.

She tossed her carefree, golden mane
With her very special flare.
She laughed and beckoned me to come,
To flee from winter's care.

How willingly I skipped behind
This vision garbed in green.
How quick my step, how light my heart,
And my spirit, how serene.

Adversity would come again,
Yet I knew throughout it all
I would grasp and hold the moment
When April came to call.

My Garden
Regina Scopelitis
Tucson, Arizona

I watch my growing garden
Where my hands have felt the sod,
And I feel a peace within me
In my communion here with God.

The lilies white with purity,
The roses red with love,
The morning glories wet with dew
And as blue as skies above.

The little purple violets,
So shy with heads bent down,
Stand by the yellow daffodils,
Who proudly wear their crown.

I've spent such happy hours
Bringing flowers from the sod.
I love my growing garden,
Kissed by angels, blessed by God.

Spring's Sonnet

Irene Leland
St. Louis, Missouri

When nature rings the bells
    that toll the spring
And spreads her news throughout
    the land and air,
The birds awake with glory, and they bring
A song of welcome for all life to share.

The flowers yawn and show their
    blossomed buds
In grace and tribute to the praised resound.
Earth's hardened crust receives the sun above
And bids goodbye to frost that leaves
    her ground.

And as the season's bloom returns anew,
I, too, rejoice the fresh and fragrant spell;
Yet with no song, no scent, pied hue,
How can I worship in a way as well?

While nature shifts with spring, the same
    I'll be;
For all my laud I'll hold inside of me.

Spring Flowers

Myrle Glace
Upper Holland, Pennsylvania

Of all the flowers that bloom in spring
I think there's none so fair
As the shy and dainty violet
With its color soft and rare.

The daffodil is light and gay
As her colors brightly show.
And then there is the tulip,
Tall, vivid, all aglow.

Forsythia is lovely,
But looks better from afar.
And daisies, ah, fresh daisies
In the field or in a jar.

Oh well, I could go on and on;
There's some I can't recall.
And actually, the simple truth,
I think I love them all.

Editor's Note: Readers are invited to submit unpublished, original poetry for possible publication in future issues of Ideals. *Please send typed copies only; manuscripts will not be returned. Writers receive $10 for each published submission. Send material to Readers' Reflections, Ideals Publications, Inc., P.O. Box 305300, Nashville, Tennessee 37230-5300.*

April

Margaret Rorke

They call their baby "April."
Oh, what a lovely name!
It conjures up a picture
Too free to fit a frame:

A dainty little blossom—
A tiny crocus bud—
That pushes past dissuasion
To part the melting mud;

A timid, furry bunny;
A yellow-feathered chick;
A glimpse of green transfusing
What had appeared a stick;

A robin brightly breasted
A-singing to the sky
As if to ask for color
To use for eggshell dye;

A branch of pussy willow;
A brook with babbling tongue;
A lambkin in a meadow—
Just all that's fresh and young.

They call their baby "April,"
The month of hope and cheer.
How nice to carry April
Around with one all year!

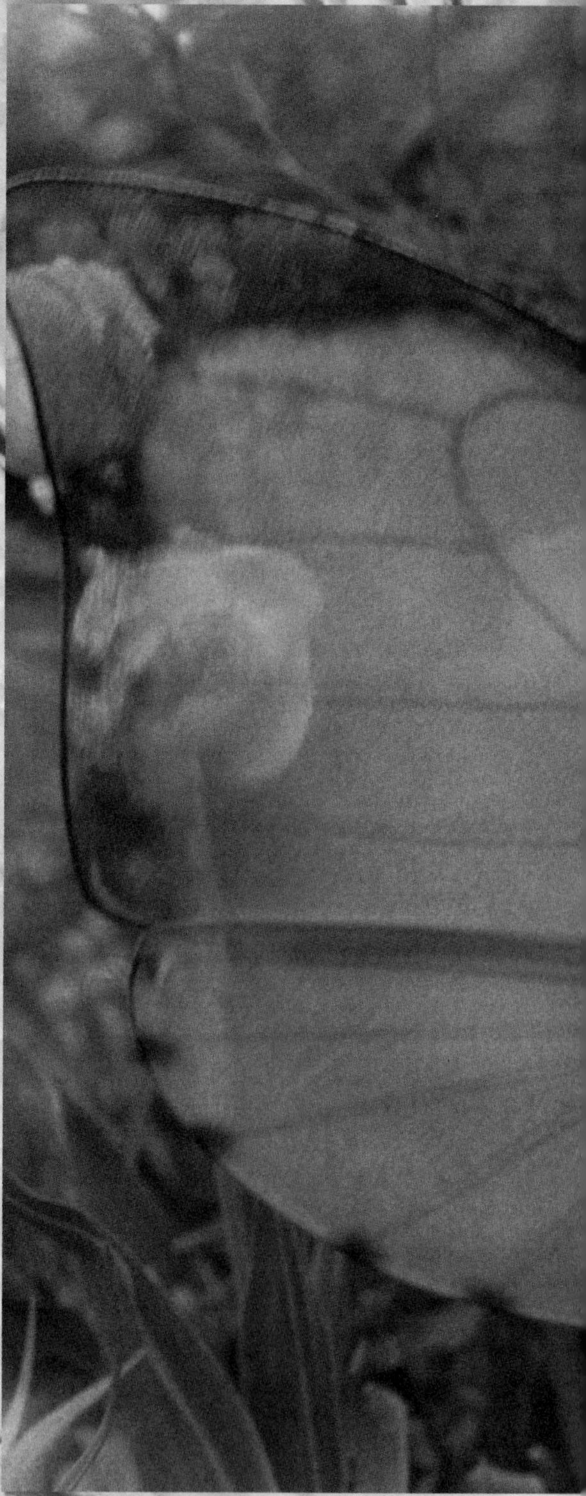

*The essence of childhood is wrapped up in one wondrous
grin. Photo by Michele-Salmieri/FPG International.*

April

Jean S. Platt

If asked to describe her, I guess I would say
less restless than March, less placid than May,
with robins appearing again on the sill
and yellow forsythia high on the hill.

If asked to describe her, I guess I would tell
of bright golden daffodils down by the dell,

of blossoms beginning to bloom on the trees
and heavenly fragrance adrift on the breeze;
of lambs in the meadow and foals in the glen—
a world, winter-weary, reviving again.

If asked to describe her, how could I impart
the wonder that April evokes in my heart?

A SLICE OF LIFE

Edgar A. Guest

I BELIEVE

I believe in friendship, and I believe in trees,
And I believe in hollyhocks a-swaying in the breeze,
And I believe in robins and roses white and red
And rippling brooks and rivers and blue skies
    overhead,
And I believe in laughter, and I believe in love,
And I believe the daffodils believe in God above.

I am no unbeliever. I know that men are true;
I know the joy of summertime when skies above
    are blue;
I know there is no earthly power can shape
    a budding rose
Or bring a daisy into bloom; with all that

wisdom knows,
It could not fashion, if it would, the humblest
    blade of grass
Or stretch a living carpet where the weary
    travelers pass.

I believe in friendship, for I have found it good.
And I believe in kindly words, for I have understood;
My faith is founded on the years and all
    that I have seen,
Something of God I've looked upon no matter where
    I've been.
Within a swamp but yesterday, a lily smiled at me,
And only God could set it there to bloom for me to see.

Edgar A. Guest began his illustrious career in 1895 at the age of fourteen when his work first appeared in the Detroit Free Press. *His column was syndicated in over three hundred newspapers, and he became known as "The Poet of the People."*

Readers' Forum

Snapshots from Our Ideals *Readers*

UPPER LEFT: Mrs. Frances B. Russell of Greenville, South Carolina, tells us she keeps this snapshot of her great-grandchildren at the breakfast table to help her start each day with a smile. Two-and-a-half-year-old Russell is giving his little sister, Anna, age six months, a hug amid the blooms at the Holy Trinity Church in Clemson. Russell and Anna are the children of Mike and Angie Newton.

LOWER LEFT: Grandma Marcia Hancock of Shoreline, Washington, believes this candid photo of her two granddaughters was even better than the posed shots of the two girls in their Easter finery. Lara Curry, age three, and Linsey Curry, age one and a half, were caught taking a break to explore the goodies in their Easter baskets.

UPPER RIGHT: Hayley Sparler seems to think even chilly Easter Sundays can be enjoyable. The photo was sent to us by Hayley's great-grandmother, Martha Dawson of Squaw Valley, California, who wrote a poem describing the day and how "In her hat with trim/ Hayley was a hymn/ script on gold leaf."

BELOW RIGHT: In 1954, Susan Denbo Gladieux and her brother took time to smell the tulips and pose for this photo for their father, Jerald Denbo. Susan, who now lives in Bakersfield, California, sent the snapshot to us and explained that her parents have loved *Ideals* for many years and would love to see this vintage shot reprinted in the magazine.

Thank you Mrs. Frances B. Russell, Marcia Hancock, Martha Dawson, and Susan Denbo Gladieux for sharing your family photographs with *Ideals*. We hope to hear from other readers who would like to share snapshots with the *Ideals* family. Please include a self-addressed, stamped envelope if you would like the photos returned. Keep your original photographs for safekeeping and send duplicate photos along with your name, address, and telephone number to:

Readers' Forum
Ideals Publications Inc.
P.O. Box 305300
Nashville, Tennessee 37230

ideals

Publisher, Patricia A. Pingry
Editor, Michelle Prater Burke
Designer, Travis Rader
Copy Editor, Elizabeth Kea
Contributing Editors, Lansing Christman, Deana Deck, Pamela Kennedy, and Nancy Skarmeas

ACKNOWLEDGMENTS

DICKINSON, EMILY. "Dear March." Reprinted by permission of the publishers and the Trustees of Amherst College from *The Poems of Emily Dickinson,* Ralph W. Franklin, ed., Cambridge, Mass.: The Belknap Press of Harvard University Press, Copyright © 1998 by the President and Fellows of Harvard College. Copyright © 1951, 1955, 1979 by the President and Fellows of Harvard College. GUEST, EDGAR. "I Believe" from *The Light of Faith.* Reprinted by permission of Henry Sobell, Jr. HOLMES, MARJORIE. An excerpt from "The Mail Order Catalog" from *You and I and Yesterday* by Marjorie Holmes. Reprinted by permission of the author. MURTON, JESSIE WILMORE. "April Rain" from *The Shining Thread* by Jessie Wilmore Murton. Reprinted by permission of Pacific Press Publishing Association. RORKE, MARGARET. "April" from *An Old Cracked Cup* by Margaret Rorke. Reprinted by permission of the author. SPENCER, ANNE BETHEL. "Easter Eve" used by permission of the author's estate. TREMBLE, STELLA. "Spring Rain" from *Thorns and Thistledown* by Stella Tremble. Reprinted by permission of Trueman Tremble. WATKINS, GRACE V. "Cathedrals." Reprinted by courtesy of *War Cry Magazine.* Our sincere thanks to the following authors whom we were unable to locate: Sylvia Trent Auxier for "April Rain at Night" and Sheila Stinson for "I Shall Build a House" and "Spring Road."

BEAUTY OF A SPRING MORNING

George R. Kossik

The rising sun from out the east
Is playing on the hills,
Where morning's dawn lies softly on
Bright beds of daffodils.

In fragrant meadows filled with flowers
The happy songbirds sing,
Their merry throats composing notes
Full of the joy of spring.

Sweet is the murmur of the stream
There in the vale below,
A crystal glide that glows and gleams
With sweet incessant flow.

This lovely morn of beauties rare
Will in my heart abide,
And this I pray this bright spring day:
May I be thus inside.

THE BIRTH OF SPRING

Gertrude Rudberg

Today I'll watch the pink spring sky
Beyond the mountains, snowcapped high.
I'll see the leafless trees so bare
Swell up their buds to kiss the air.

I'll see the snowdrifts melt away
To find the spring earth greenish gray,
And in my garden I will have found
Some tiny shoots that prick the ground.

I'll see the river's mighty flow
Go rolling on in silver glow,
And in the woodlands I shall hear
The tiny brooklet's happy cheer.

I'll see the flames redden the sky
As lacy clouds go slowly by,
And as the sun warms up the earth
I'll know that spring has given birth.

UNITED STATES POSTAL SERVICE • REQUIRED BY 39 U.S.C. 3685 • STATEMENT OF OWNERSHIP, MANAGEMENT, AND CIRCULATION 1. Publication Title: Ideals. 2. Publication No.: 0019-137X. 3. Filing Date: 9/27/99. 4. Issue Frequency: 6 times a year, January, March, May, July, September, and November. 5. No. of Issues Published Annually: Six. 6. Annual Subscription Price: $19.95. 7. Complete Mailing Address of Known Office of Publication: 535 Metroplex Dr., Ste. 250, PO Box 305300, Davidson County, Nashville, TN 37230-5300. 8. Complete Mailing Address of Headquarters or General Business Office of Publisher: 535 Metroplex Dr., Ste. 250, PO Box 305300, Davidson County, Nashville, TN 37230-5300. 9. Full Names and Complete Mailing Addresses of Publisher, Editor, and Managing Editor: Publisher: Patricia A. Pingry, 535 Metroplex Dr., Ste. 250, Nashville, TN 37211; Editor: Michelle Prater Burke, 535 Metroplex Dr., Ste. 250, Nashville, TN 37211; Managing Editor: Michelle Prater Burke, 535 Metroplex Dr., Ste. 250, Nashville, TN 37211. 10. Owner (Full Name and Complete Mailing Address): Ideals Publications Incorporated, 535 Metroplex Dr., Ste. 250, Nashville, TN 37211. Stockholders Owning or Holding 1 Percent or More of Total Amount of Stock: Simon Waterlow, President, 535 Metroplex Dr., Ste. 250, Nashville, TN 37211; Marty Flanagan, Vice President, Finance, 535 Metroplex Dr., Ste. 250, Nashville, TN 37211. 11. Known Bondholders, Mortgagees, and Other Security Holders Owning or Holding 1 Percent or More of Total Amount of Bonds, Mortgages, or Other Securities: Egmont Foundation, Vognmagergade II, 1148 Copenhagen K, Denmark and First Star Bank, 814 Church Street, Nashville, TN 37203. 12. For completion by nonprofit organizations authorized to mail at special rates: Not Applicable. 13. Publication Title: Ideals. 14. Issue Date for Circulation Data Below: Friendship, July 1999. 15. Extent and Nature of Circulation: Average No. Copies Each Issue During Preceding 12 Months: A. Total No. Copies (Net Press Run): 211,788. B. Paid and/or Requested Circulation: (1) Paid/Requested Outside-County Mail Subscriptions: 166,028. (2) Paid In-County Subscriptions: 0. (3) Sales Through Dealers and Carriers, Street Vendors, and Counter Sales: 22,591. (4) Other Classes Mailed Through the USPS: 0. C. Total Paid and/or Requested Circulation: 188,619. D. Free Distribution by Mail: 0. E. Free Distribution Outside the Mail: 0. F. Total Free Distribution: 0. G. Total Distribution: 188,619. H. Copies not Distributed: 23,169. I. Total: 211,788. Percent Paid and/or Requested Circulation: 100%. No. Copies of Single Issue Published Nearest to Filing Date: A. Total No. Copies (Net Press Run): 168,198. Paid and/or Requested Circulation: (1) Paid/Requested Outside-County Mail Subscriptions: 150,732. (2) Paid In-County Subscriptions: 0. (3) Sales Through Dealers and Carriers, Street Vendors, and Counter Sales: 9,669. (4) Other Classes Mailed Through the USPS: 0. C. Total Paid and/or Requested Circulation: 160, 401. D. Free Distribution by Mail: 0. E. Free Distribution Outside the Mail: 0. F. Total Free Distribution: 0. G. Total Distribution: 160,401. H. Copies Not Distributed: 7,797. I. Total: 168,198. Percent Paid and/or Requested Circulation: 100%. I certify that all information furnished is true and complete. Rose A. Yates, Vice President, Systems and Operations